INVENTING THE
TELEVISION

Published by The Child's World®
1980 Lookout Drive • Mankato, MN 56003-1705
800-599-READ • www.childsworld.com

Acknowledgments
The Child's World®: Mary Berendes, Publishing Director
Red Line Editorial: Design, editorial direction, and production
Photographs ©: Vita Khorzhevska/Shutterstock Images, cover, 1; Russell Lee/Library
of Congress, 4; Harris & Ewing/Library of Congress, 7; Bettmann/Corbis, 8, 13, 14, 17;
Hulton-Deutsch Collection/Corbis, 11; SuperStock/Corbis, 18; Harold M. Lambert/
Getty Images, 20

ISBN 9781634074612

LCCN 2015946289

Printed in the United States of America
Mankato, MN
December, 2015
PA02284

ABOUT THE AUTHOR

Carolee Laine is an educator and children's writer. She has written social
studies textbooks, educational materials, and passages for statewide
assessments. She enjoys learning through researching and writing nonfiction
books for young readers. Carolee lives in the Chicago suburbs.

TABLE OF
CONTENTS

Chapter 1

A TIME BEFORE TELEVISION

After dinner, the family gathered in the living room. Dad fiddled with a knob on the radio for a few seconds. Then, their favorite cowboy show came in loud and clear. It was 1940.

The family listened to *The Lone Ranger*. The masked hero captured outlaws who had robbed a bank. Then he rode away on his horse, Silver. None of the other characters knew who the Lone Ranger was. In their living room, the family's imaginations helped them picture the scene. Sound effects made it seem like Silver really was galloping across the plains.

At other times, the family cheered their favorite baseball team. A sports announcer described every play. They could hear the crack of the bat as it hit the ball. They could imagine the player running the bases.

◄ A man and his daughter listen to the radio in 1940.

Dad laughed at his favorite comedy shows. He repeated the jokes to his friends. Mom listened to popular singers and sang along with the latest songs. Teenagers danced to the music of big bands that were hundreds of miles away. Children tried to solve mysteries along with their favorite detectives.

Listeners depended on evening news reports to learn about world events. Many Americans tuned in when President Franklin Roosevelt spoke on the radio. It was like having the president in their living room!

Radios kept people informed and entertained. The technology was great, but it was limited. People wanted more. In movie theaters, they could hear sounds and see moving pictures at the same time. Why couldn't they do that in their own homes?

To some people, watching moving pictures in their homes seemed like a dream. They thought it could never happen. But others believed it could. And they worked toward that goal. Television sets did not become widely used until the 1950s. But the amazing story behind the invention of television began many years earlier.

President Roosevelt gives a speech from his desk ▶
at the White House.

TWO IMPORTANT INVENTORS

While growing up in Scotland in the late 1800s, John Logie Baird had a good imagination. He was often sick as a child, so he had to stay at home. It was not much fun being alone all day. He set up a telephone system to connect his home to other homes nearby. Then he could talk to his friends.

As an adult, Baird came up with ideas for many inventions. There was just one problem. Some of his inventions didn't work! For example, he developed a razor made of glass. When he tested it, he cut himself badly. Later, he got a job as a city engineer. But one of his inventions blew out much of the city's power supply. Baird was fired.

Baird invented socks that kept feet dry. He invented soap for cleaning floors. He enjoyed some success selling these products. But he was not satisfied. He had read about a new idea called

◄ **Baird works on his early television.**

television. And he kept thinking about it. Baird used the money from his businesses to follow his dream of inventing television.

He gathered objects from around his house. Then he put them together with glue and string. Finally, his invention was ready for a test. Would it work? Baird watched nervously. A cardboard disk spun like a pinwheel around a knitting needle. The disk picked up light and sent it to a battery cell. The cell produced an electric current. The current sent light patterns to another spinning disk. Then the patterns appeared on a screen 2 feet (.6 m) away. Baird smiled with relief. He had done it!

At first, Baird's television showed only shadowy shapes. By 1925, he figured out a way to improve it. But he needed another person to help test the new invention. He raced outside his office and convinced a boy to help him. He paid the boy to sit in front of the **transmitter**. The boy's face clearly showed on the screen. It was the first human face ever seen on television. "I could scarcely believe my eyes!" Baird later said.[1]

On the other side of the ocean, others were working on the same idea. Philo Farnsworth grew up in a log cabin in Utah in the early 1900s. The cabin had no radio, telephone, or lights. Life changed when Farnsworth's family moved to a farm in Idaho. The house had electricity! It also had a stack of science magazines left behind by another family.

▲ Baird sits by his transmitter.

Farnsworth spent hours reading about science. Like Baird, he read about television. One day when Farnsworth was plowing fields, the straight rows gave him an idea. He thought he could change pictures into straight lines of light. He could use electricity to send light to a **receiver**. The lines of light could be put back together on a screen. Then people could view the pictures. Could he really make this idea work?

As an adult, Farnsworth borrowed money and moved to California. In 1926, he set up a laboratory and began working on his idea. The process required three parts. A camera turned pictures into a **signal**. A transmitter sent the signal through the air or through wires. A receiver turned the signal back into a picture.

Farnsworth's first attempts failed. He had to borrow more money to keep trying. By 1928, he made the first electronic television. It did not have moving parts like the one Baird had invented. Farnsworth's television was based on an idea he had sketched in his high school science class. And it worked!

Farnsworth adjusts a dial on an early television. ▶

Chapter 3

THE RACE TO INVENT TELEVISION

In 1934, crowds passed a camera on their way into an exhibit in Philadelphia, Pennsylvania. People were amazed to see themselves on a television screen nearby. Inside the building, people excitedly watched a 12-inch (30-cm) screen. They saw trained dogs, tennis players, and dancers that were in another room. They were seeing Farnsworth's invention for the first time.

Farnsworth believed he had the rights to the first electronic television. But another inventor, Vladimir Zworykin, also claimed the rights to the invention. Zworykin was born in Russia. In college, he had studied science with a professor who made an early television. Zworykin moved to the United States and worked for RCA, a large electronics company.

Zworykin developed a television camera. His camera was similar to the one Farnsworth invented. For many years,

◀ Zworykin (left) shows a woman how his television works.

Farnsworth and Zworykin battled in court. Zworykin received credit for his work. But the **patent**, or right to the invention, was awarded to Farnsworth.

Companies started to realize there was money to be made by selling television sets for homes. But people were not very interested in buying them. David Sarnoff was the president of RCA. He knew just what to do. He would use a big event to attract a lot of attention.

Sarnoff used the 1939 World's Fair in New York, which was the biggest event of its time. The fair was called World of Tomorrow. What a perfect place to introduce the wonders of television! Opening day was a sunny Sunday in April. Thousands of people streamed through the fair's gates. The fairgoers were delighted by the exhibits that gave them a peek into the future.

The crowd cheered and clapped when President Roosevelt gave a speech. A huge parade and music added to the excitement. Just as Sarnoff had planned, the whole thing was shown on television.

People stood in long lines to get into the RCA display. They took turns watching the fair on tiny screens that were 3 inches (8 cm) wide and 2 inches (5 cm) tall. One visitor said, "I can't believe it! I must be dreaming."[2]

▲ A televised image of Roosevelt's speech
at the 1939 World's Fair

Sarnoff knew people would not buy television sets unless there was something interesting to watch. So he announced a new lineup of programs. Television stations began to show baseball games, football games, and boxing matches. Sports **broadcasts** became popular programs.

Television sales were not as good as Sarnoff had expected. But he didn't give up. "There's a vast market out there, and we're going to capture it," he said.[3]

Chapter 4

HOW TELEVISION CHANGED LIFE

The kids heard the familiar theme song. They ran to sit in front of the television set and watch *Walt Disney's Wonderful World of Color*. The program entertained the whole family. Sometimes it showed cartoons. At other times it featured programs about nature, history, or adventure.

It was the 1960s. By now, color television sets were becoming common. The television set was the most important piece of furniture in the living room. It was the only television in the house. Television offered something for everyone. Young children watched shows that helped them learn letters, numbers, and colors. Teenagers rushed home from school to watch a popular dance show. They learned the latest dances. They practiced dancing to the newest songs.

◄ By the 1960s, most homes in the United States had a television.

▲ A family watches television in the 1960s.

Adults watched programs that helped them decide who to vote for in a presidential election. Then they watched the new president take the **oath** of office.

Moms watched commercials and learned about new products. Sometimes **sponsors** made ads that appealed to children. The kids begged their parents to buy something they had seen on television.

By the 1960s, television provided most people with information and entertainment. It gave people up-to-the-minute news reports. It allowed people to see different countries. And the viewers didn't even have to leave their homes!

In 1940, most people could not even imagine having a television set in their home. By 1960, most people had a television. But they could not imagine remote controls, flat screens, and video games. Today, those things are common. Television has come a long way since it was invented. It's hard to imagine what television will be like in the future!

COMPARING TELEVISION PAST AND PRESENT

	1950	2015
number of television stations	fewer than 100	more than 1,300
average time spent watching television every day	4 hours, 35 minutes	5 hours, 11 minutes
number of homes with television sets	9 of every 100	99 of every 100

GLOSSARY

broadcasts (BRAWD-kasts): Broadcasts are radio or television programs. Millions of people watch television news broadcasts.

oath (OHTH): An oath is a promise. The president takes an oath to uphold the laws of the United States.

patent (PAT-nt): A patent is the legal right to make, use, and sell an invention. The government awarded Farnsworth a patent for his invention.

receiver (ri-SEE-vur): A receiver is a device that changes electric signals into sound or pictures. A radio's receiver is what turns signals into sounds that people can hear.

signal (SIG-nuhl): A signal is a sound or a picture that is sent through the air or wires to a television set. The early television signal could only reach homes around large cities.

sponsors (SPON-surz): Sponsors are people or groups that pay for the cost of something. Sponsors pay television stations to show advertisements during shows.

transmitter (tranz-MIT-uhr): A transmitter is something that sends a signal. A transmitter sends a television signal to a home.

TO LEARN MORE

Books

Cupp, Dave, and Cecilia Minden. *Television Reporters.* Mankato, MN: The Child's World, 2014.

Hirschmann, Kris. *HDTV: High Definition Television.* Chicago: Norwood House, 2011.

Krull, Kathleen. *The Boy Who Invented TV: The Story of Philo Farnsworth.* New York: Alfred A. Knopf, 2009.

Richter, Joanne. *Inventing the Television.* New York: Crabtree, 2006.

Web Sites

Visit our Web site for links about television: childsworld.com/links

Note to Parents, Teachers, and Librarians: We routinely verify our Web links to make sure they are safe and active sites. So encourage your readers to check them out!

SOURCE NOTES

1. Daniel Stashower. *The Boy Genius and the Mogul: The Untold Story of Television.* New York: Broadway Books, 2002. Print. 66–67.

2. Elliott Kalan. "(Tele)Visions of Tomorrow." *World's Fair: Enter the World of Tomorrow.* New York Public Library, n.d. Web. 11 Jun. 2015.

3. Evan I. Schwartz. *The Last Lone Inventor: A Tale of Genius, Deceit, and the Birth of Television.* New York: HarperCollins, 2002. Print. 281.

INDEX